A speaking silence

A speaking silence
Quaker poets of today

edited by R V Bailey and Stevie Krayer

Indigo Dreams Publishing

First Edition: A Speaking Silence: Quaker poets of today
First published in Great Britain in 2013 by:
Indigo Dreams Publishing
24 Forest Houses
Cookworthy Moor
Halwill
Beaworthy
Devon
EX21 5UU

www.indigodreams.co.uk

ISBN 978-1-909357-30-3

British Library Cataloguing in Publication Data. A CIP record for this book can be obtained from the British Library.

Designed and typeset in Palatino Linotype by Indigo Dreams.
Front cover: 'The Rowan Tree' by Anne Gregson
www.littlewedlockgallery.co.uk

Printed and bound in Great Britain by Imprint Academic, Exeter.

Papers used by Indigo Dreams are recyclable products made from wood grown in sustainable forests following the guidance of the Forest Stewardship Council.

Contents

7

Introduction

Judging by the flood of submissions we had for this anthology, there seems to be an affinity between poetry and Quakerism. Perhaps it's the effect of worshipping in the manner of Friends. Quietening one's busy mind and restless body in order to listen to the 'still, small voice' is also an excellent way to let the Muse make contact.

Quakers haven't always been very encouraging to poets, or to artists in general, thinking that time spent on such things was wasted when there was so much to be done in reclaiming the world for God. But attitudes have long since changed: 'God is in all beauty' as Caroline Graveson sturdily said, in 1937, 'not only in the natural beauty of earth and sky, but in all fitness of language and rhythm...whether it describe a Hamlet or a Falstaff'. Far more Quaker poets than we'd expected responded to our initial invitation in *The Friend,* and it has been quite a challenge, as well as a pleasure, to select the poems included here.

Poetry is about trying to tell the truth, which is not easy: truth is not the same as 'facts'. It comes in many shapes, and is, among other things, a matter of the imagination – which is also poetry's territory. We do well to take the imagination seriously: it is where everything begins, from the mystic's vision to the torturer's ingenuity. If we never fell in love, or suffered loss or death or loneliness or any of the great human experiences, perhaps we wouldn't need poetry.

These are poems by Quakers, or by those who feel most at home in Quaker Meetings. But it's not a collection of poems about specifically Quaker subjects, nor does it offer explicit Quaker attitudes – though a thoughtful reader may well discern in the poems echoes of what might be called a Quaker sensibility. There is a common misperception that Quakers are frightfully *good* – with a bit of emphasis on the 'frightful'. We

11

hope this selection of poems will demonstrate that Quakers are human, with the same organs, dimensions, affections and passions as the rest of humanity. We were looking above all for good poets, who wrote well about whatever came their way, so you'll find a wide variety of topics, as well as a variety of voices and approaches and styles, both formal and experimental.

It's a characteristic of Friends that we make no distinction between the sacred and the everyday. By the same token, Quaker poets – in common with most modern poets – make no distinction between subjects. Poets write about everything: there are no 'poetic' subjects. Critics at different times have tried to make rules about this, but poets promptly go off and break them. Nothing is too big or too small: poetry accepts both Hamlet and Falstaff. The editors themselves have differing personal tastes, and that itself has added a further dizzying dimension to the collection.

Poetry has been described as organised violence committed on everyday language: it's full of rule-breaking; it's a professional act of resistance, subversive, unexpected (so Quakers should feel at home with poetry). English is a double-jointed language, and poetry stretches it to the limits. The ambiguity, the readiness to contradict itself, the apparent insanity, the force of the smallest words like *to, by, of* – all these are part of the combination of English and poetry. So we looked for poems that are alive, that have this kind of energy about them. And we looked for poets who trust their readers, who suggest more than they say, who have a way with language that is individual and fresh.

We hoped to find words being pushed to their extreme, being considered lovingly for each facet – for their looks, their sounds, their precise places – as if they were potential ballet-dancers. We looked for poets who have a good ear, who could relate the pattern of what they're saying to the pattern of how they say it. We looked for good beginnings, that pull the reader in; and for good endings, that know when to stop, and how. We hoped, too, for wit. And we looked for recognisably contemporary voices, not just decorative language, or those familiar metres which – while splendidly suited to their own particular century – seem not to belong in ours.

Most of the writers are alive today; a handful are only fairly recently dead. Some are famous; many are not – yet. In keeping with the traditional Quaker principles of equality and simplicity, we haven't segregated the eminent from the obscure; all the poets appear in straightforward alphabetical order.

Poetry is for real people, not just for other poets, so it should be accessible, even though it may require some effort in reading. Sometimes poetry deals with subjects that are just too difficult to write about very simply. But (you guessed it) we haven't much sympathy with the portentous. It's no good being 'deep and meaningful' if what you write isn't meaningful to anybody else.

It was exciting that we found these qualities in so many poets, and we are very grateful to them for their generosity in allowing us to include their work. We hope that you, our readers, will find poems here that will both delight you and make you think.

R V Bailey
Stevie Krayer

13

Jo Alberti

Forgetting

You are walking down the road,
you are on my doorstep.
Forgetting the years between
I see an old man.

We climbed that hill
together – so you tell me.
I hear the story
as if another's tale.

I believed in God back then
and love that lasted.
I no longer breathe
such absolute air.

Pain spilled, when you left –
so my journal tells me.
Now I am veined
with contentment.

A swallow lectures me from the wires
my throat is caught in her song.
How many such ecstasies
sing me to joy, then fade?

Gillian Allnutt

the shawl
(i.m. Julia Darling)

of air and wool

her frail earthwhile

who promised her people

palanquin, purple and pall

and left them all

a little something fit for April

snowfall

The Road Home

It is the road to God
that matters now, the ragged road, the wood.

And if you will, drop pebbles here and there
like Hansel, Gretel, right where

they'll shine
in the wilful light of the moon.

You won't be going back to the hut
where father, mother plot

the *cul de sac* of the world
in a field

that's permanently full
of people

looking for a festival
of literature, a fairy tale,

a feathered
nest of brothers, sisters. Would

that first world, bared now to the word
God, wade

with you, through wood, into the weald and weather
of the stars?

Angela Arnold

Inhabiting the Door

Settling mid-doorway, middle
of the day: splintered view,
off-centre feeling.
Doing the hard-floor shuffle.
Doing *dislocated*.
Doing *raw*.
Not doing any doing.
Taking liberties with life, being
door yourself now
for long unmoments, properly
grateful
for nothing at all.

Bryan Aspden 1933-1999

Nant Honddu
(for David Jones)

A grail of gorse; basketwork hedges
Threaded with birds. It's the end of March;
Spring still an outline map. These windflowers
And a purse of woodsorrel all that's filled in –

Two memories merging from the same month
Ten years apart, and at different ends of the path
That crosses your land and marks its eastern border.
When you were here you painted two black ponies

Grazing in a cup of the hills; a wattle fence;
Lopped ash and oak; a coverlet of fields;
Forestry rising to the shaved head of the moor –
A land man had neighboured long enough

To turn its grudge to giving – though the gifts
Weren't even-handed, nor was the taking.
You hankered for its comfort, grown up away.
After the first war came here to paint, to study, to recover.

You painted the river coming from Penny Beacon
Or Hay Bluff, past Capel-y-Ffin, Pont-y-Wyrlod
To Garn Farm, Dôl Alice, Crucorney
Where three centuries of change have got their tongues

Round the place names, and Englished but not misplaced
                                                        them.
Ten years ago I drove the Austin Cambridge
By the side of Nant Honddu, parked where the sign
Pointed a peglegged walker over Hatterall Hill

Away from Wales, to Hereford cattle and apples.
Today in the wind's gap above Bodfari I watch
Sheep, a sheepdog, two ponies, try to learn
Like you 'the creatureliness of things'; find
Some kindly forms, words that would heal the hurt
Of this land with its boundary in its heart.

Stonecrop

Below a row of houses
Thatched with stars
The quarry path trudging off

Without a word
From lungs that test
The surgeon's knife

In stone fields
The chough reaps
With its red sickle

There's a small bitter flower
On a stem of wire
Beaded with pebbles

That has no need to migrate
Having learned to cadge
A drink from slate.

Elizabeth Bailey

Martha's song

"That good part?"
Listen.

I've stirred ferment in the pot,
Drawn conclusions from the well,

Regularly gathered straying thoughts,
Religiously polished reflections,

Woven stories   unpicked dreams

Spun philosophies on to the spindle

Weeded out fears   sown hopes.

Desires nursed fluttering in cupped hands
Prayers rising under the warm cloth.

And all the while I tend the
Flickering silence within.

Think on.
We are one.

R V Bailey

With You

I stand with you in the garden
The birds' surprising madrigals
Rise through the roar of bees.

I stand with you in the kitchen
Dear damaged long loved over-used
Pans and pots protect us.

I stand with you in the hallway
With the deep oak tick of the clock
And the turning stair.

We sit by books in the lamplight
Importunate nondescript dog and cat
Surround us warmly.

We lie in the lofty bedroom
The church clock through the window
Quartering Gloucestershire silences.

Without you, no garden.
Sunshine withers on the plum tree
House shrinks derelict into dust.

Cautious

There are other conversations we might have had,
As we met on the hill: the one about Mr Brown,
Or the new gate. But we talk about the weather,
As usual, and whether his washing will get wet.

There are other ways home I could have taken:
Through the houses, perhaps, or along the main road.
But I take the usual one, through the trees,
Down the hill where the blackberries grow.

Sometimes these bits of life, unspoken, unvisited,
Move shyly forward, as if their time has come.
We take a rougher road or talk of harder things.
The going's not so easy, but the views are good.

Yet further back again, some other time, the
Dark inconceivable, the vast unimagined
Lumbers towards the light, shouldering
Certainties aside, casting new shadows.

Jennifer Barraclough

The Watch Cottage

I live in different houses now.
Bigger and busier, bought to serve an end –
Nearer to work, to roads, to friends.
They're solid houses, stone-built, gardened, groomed,
Two of us knowing how to occupy each room.

This is a house I think I might have known.

I'm eight or nine. I go through fields alone.
I find the ruins of old cottages,
Grassed over, lost, a frame, a shape.
Sometimes there's wallpaper, a grate,
Cupboards with rubble, dust.

At night my father works alone
In the small house that's now a lumber store.
He takes a Tilley lamp. It hisses through the time
We're there together, while he planes
Or handles seeds and plants.

I play upstairs, in a low room
That might have sheltered three or four, or more.
They're not here with me. This is no ghost-reviving exercise.
I'm by myself, with things that know their business,
Walls, floors, a certain kind of watchfulness.

It's cold. The winter's afternoon brings down the night.
Someone is coming in to speak to me, switch on the light.

Cutting the grass at Woodbrooke
(i.m. Jack Barraclough 1916-1991)

They've come to scythe the grass today.
All summer it's grown high and whispering.
Hot sun, the hiss of blade through stem,
The rustling push, the shimmering fall.

He turns the sickle on its end,
Bears down, and lets the whetstone slide.

A pause, and then the cut begins again.

In the bright sun, I sit beside his bed.
Each breath's pulled in; a pause; released.
I trace the papery skin, the thinning hair,
Raw in the light, am still.

The breath heaves in. The scythe blade swings.

Jackie Bartlett

Memento

After Passchendaele
he kept a bent penny in his pocket.
Picked up from the mud
it was bright

where the bullet had winged it
the king's face scarred
to an idiot's leer.

He never said much; talked only
of how time, behind the lines
dragged itself along like a hobbled mule

or stopped suddenly
just as a bell pealed from a tower somewhere
or, in the real world
somebody got born, somebody laughed,
caught a tram, lit a fag.

Alice Beer 1912-2011

On growing old

Like mice in the night
the years that pass are gnawing
at our life ahead.

Bit by bit the paths
our life takes seem narrower,
steeper and more rugged.

The ruts get deeper,
the woods more dense, the bright star
before us brighter.

De Montfort Square

Surrounded on three sides
by trees and hedges
its brightness tempered
by the dust and rain of years,
raised on a pedestal the figure of a man
who in his lifetime stood in a pulpit
preaching the joys of virtue, temperance,
of Baptist faith.

This Saturday morning
a man in crumpled clothes
waking from his befuddled dreams
to cold and damp under the hedge
where he had stumbled after a drinking session,
stands up and shouts his anger, his misery
for everyone to hear.
The trees look on – they've heard it all before.

Kathleen Bell

Aphasia

You are the tenth Muse, mistress
of stammers, gaps, misprision.

At first, we do not prize your bounty
but term it symptom, loss, disorder.

Then, dimly, we perceive your grace
in struggles to explore, to bridge the space
from mind to mind, surround
the arbitrary, inefficient sign.

As this:

"It is egg-shaped, in breadth much as a daisy,
a fruit which may be green or black
but at best red, termed 'flame'.
They do not taste of fire
but may resemble plump, rough jewels
and grow in clusters like Diana's breasts ...
The juice is well-contained, not bursting down
neck, throat and wrists in over-ripeness,
and you should take one singly in your mouth,
with teeth unpick the skin
and tease the sweetness from the flesh within,
cooling and fragrant on the tongue ...
And then, the fruit is crushed to make a drink
whose name I can't recall,
but Homer found it dark, dark as the sea."

And so we labour, reaching out
from code toward exactness,
stumbling, feeling forward, finding more
than in the quick, if apt, translation.

All this we share.

But for the self
the moment beyond words
the moment when the thing, the scene, the world
suddenly *means* no more but simply *is*.

The aetherial suspension:
Eugène to Robert-Houdin, 1870

Father, I'm writing this
in love and duty, and I don't know where I am.
No matter now. The battle's done
and I was brave, I think. At least
I didn't run. None of us ran.

Father, I am not writing this,
I can't. But once I learned – do you recall? –
to catch loose thoughts from air,
to read a woman's eyelash quiver
and scrawl a strand of scent
loose on white card. You'd blindfold me
to pluck an embryo thought
still raw, out of the back
of a man's head. Father,
you taught me this. Do you remember?

Father, I'm sending this
across torn fields, smashed villages,
through angry armies to the city where
you starve, they say. Unpick the words.

I cannot see the wound.
They tell me that it's bad
and there's no ether here.
I smell the orange that you split.
You spun the pip,
burst it to flower and fruit.
Butterflies here,
real as the ones you made,
are red and buzz like flies.

You raised my arms, laid them on poles,
muffled my face.
The ether came –
I hurt. I want to drink.
You held me up and laid me on the air.
You took the poles away.

Lay me on air now, Father.
Lay me on air.
Fill up the air with blooms
and fruit, and wings –
then gently, let me go.

Peter Bennet

Augenlicht

The place we've come to leans against the sky
and dreams the moon. A midden steams.
We start a hare. We are alive.

The roads we took were intricate
and bad. Though fearful we were not deterred.
A pale girl gathers shadows from the track.

She whispers an irrevocable word
of which no meaning will survive.
She is inured to working late.

The night is old. Her one bright eye
fades from our way. She's what she seems.
She moves the oceans when she turns her back.

Catherine Benson

Being Private

The scrabble of magpie claws stops.
Rain drums on the roof. And rain
pouring its deluge down the sloping window
wavers the garden into coloured streamers.

Birds still flit from bush to tree so close
I'm in there with them.
This shed becoming overgrown is part
of their garden. Unlike the house

where people come and go, who open windows,
empty rubbish, brush paths, weed.
In here I'm part of the garden.
Secret but not hiding. Waiting

for words that might come to explain
this feeling of otherness and sanctuary.
And the rain must be there, as important
as a curtain round a hospital bed.

Gerard Benson

And Perhaps

And perhaps this time it will be different.
Perhaps the magical kings will leave their Rolls-Royces
And walk over the mountains carrying the presents
Singing as they go, a little footsore but okay.

And perhaps the terrifying blaze in the shepherds' sky
Will not be a nuclear meltdown but an explosion of angels.
Singing not multi-million pap in three-four time
But an irresistible harmony of hosannas.

And perhaps the homeless couple in the barn
Will be welcomed into the house and lavished with gifts;
And perhaps their baby will grow up, and not be executed.
And there will be no massacre of any innocents.

And perhaps...

The Bomber

The Windrush runs through field and village
before it becomes the Thames. Clear water
with waving weeds, minnows, sticklebacks;
and where it bends, boys, swimming, splashing,
floating on their backs, diving off the bank.
That's where I learnt to swim – a frantic
doggy-paddle that just kept me buoyant
and lifted my feet from the stones at the bottom.

That summer we lay on the bank and let the sun
dry us off. We heard, one glorious afternoon,
the grumbling engines of a plane, very low.
A Flying Fortress lumbered into view,
enormous with jagged holes in its fuselage,
staggering through the air, just above the willows.
I saw blue through gaps in the wings.

Amazed, frightened, we jumped to our feet and waved,
as if our frantic waving could keep him airborne.
And the man (we could see his face),
as he steered his wreck with hopes of reaching an airfield,
waved back at the naked boys on the Windrush bank.

David Blamires

The professor of signs

My primary ability is not apparent.
Billions have vanished through my transactions,
for which crushed multitudes have had to pay,
depressed and dyslexic as they are.
I am, like Samson, eyeless in Gaza.
Who is the chairman of Failure plc,
the driver of the ghost train of constant growth?
My name is Hildebrand; I slaughtered my son.
I am intemperance, ignorance, impotence.
Where is Joseph, stepfather of Joshua,
keeper of paradoxes,
the law and the lawbreaker?
I am the muse of forgotten history.
Nebuchadnezzar was put out to grass.
I am an orchestra of wounded pride.
I am the professor of signs,
  accidental rather than perspicacious.
I held back my question at the Grail castle.
My name is Romulus or perhaps Remus.
I am the sibyl of the oracles.
I am the tester of time.
I am, sadly, not unique.
Vacant possession is my hobby,
wistfulness my besetting sin.
I am the Xanthippe of wives.
I am the snows of yesteryear.
I am the zeugmas of your lives.

Basil Bunting 1900-1985

What the Chairman told Tom

Poetry? It's a hobby.
I run model trains.
Mr Shaw there breeds pigeons.

It's not work. You don't sweat.
Nobody pays for it.
You *could* advertise soap.

Art, that's opera; or repertory –
The Desert Song.
Nancy was in the chorus.

But to ask for twelve pounds a week –
married, aren't you? –
you've got a nerve.

How could I look a bus conductor
in the face
if I paid you twelve pounds?

Who says it's poetry, anyhow?
My ten year old
can do it *and* rhyme.

I get three thousand and expenses,
a car, vouchers,
but I'm an accountant.

They do what I tell them,
my company.
What do *you* do?

Nasty little words, nasty long words,
it's unhealthy.
I want to wash when I meet a poet.

They're Reds, addicts,
all delinquents.
What you write is rot.

Mr Hines says so, and he's a schoolteacher,
he ought to know.
Go and find *work*.

At Briggflatts Meetinghouse

Boasts time mocks cumber Rome. Wren
set up his own monument.
Others watch fells dwindle, think
the sun's fires sink.

Stones indeed sift to sand, oak
blends with saints' bones.
Yet for a little longer here
stone and oak shelter

silence while we ask nothing
but silence. Look how clouds dance
under the wind's wing, and leaves
delight in transience.

Robbie Burton

Knowing

He knew himself
by the coffee aisle, by the way
his feet stopped beside
dark roast espresso.

He knew himself
by the diesel pump, by his waiting
for the hose to click
whatever price on the dial.

He knew himself
by roundabouts, by the way
his grass grew no different
from his neighbours'.

Now he knows
straggled hedgerows
and the sky looking up at him
from puddles in the lane.

He's sitting on a hilltop
squinting at seven counties
smiling at the minute
he forgot himself.

Helena Chambers

On Church Street, Tewkesbury

His scalp looks tender, whelped by a razor
into raw air; the black Mohican's sparse,
but two proud inches of caterpillar
spikes – one prick and a princess could tumble
into sleep for centuries. His mid-blue fleece
is zipped tight with teeth of chrome; at the back
in letters of gold that swirl like Arabic
the words 'Suzuki + Rizla' tell the street
of his allegiances. One of his hands holds

a woman's; she (chunky beads, jeans,
hand-knitted cardigan) halts her stroll
at the jeweller's noughts and crosses pane.
Looks. No pull, no summoning of patience,
but their arms close from V to solid I
as he leans in, curious budgie at a mirror,
looking through his reflection to the shine
she wants him to see. Who's a lovely boy?
Oh, but it's you, my you, you really are.

The Lost Boys

At night they fly like Peter Pan,
drifting over towers where the lifts smell of piss,
houses where the gardens are tended.

In daylight they know one another
though all of them are strangers.
Cheek-bones are pebbles

under skin of water; in their choir
every opened mouth shows gaps.
Heroin's a fairy: she's collecting their teeth.

Wendy cannot guess what will bring the lost boys home.

Jenny Chantler

Taking a risk

Wake up one morning
and resolve to be mad
Decide to risk all
for the first or the next time
stake yourself out
as a target of love

Start by stripping
your skin off
over your head
twisting the ends
and letting it fall
in an unbroken rustle
on to the floor

Step out and
stand upright
in what now remains
the quivering rawness
live-wired and unearthed
exposed to whatever
might wander along

After small biting things
proddings and jeers
from close passers by
maybe teasing blue bruises
rips and then tears
jagged sharp ice shards
or sun crackled sky

you might be amazed
when a glory of song
climbs suddenly lark-winged
up through the blueness
clothing your gasping
with softness of down
and salving your throat
with a gush
of sweet rain

Anne Cluysenaar

Always

'*Always there is much more happening than we can bear*' –
Tomas Tranströmer.

Why, reading this, remember so suddenly,
in the glass tank, a sea anemone?
For many years, the sight must have hidden
somewhere in my brain, but now, here,

it is. And, if I don't look far,
if I forget where I stand, just enjoy
where it clings, that wavering water,
as if, beyond, some ocean moves vast,

if I do that, I won't notice the pumps
behind that little rock, its electric bubbles –
absence of others, absence of danger,
absence of turning tides, of moonlight.

Chunk of salt water. So here I stand, wanting,
again, to acquire it – like a little poem
cut off from the rest of language, except
if, turning the page, someone reads it to someone.

There were dark leaves spread out

There were dark leaves spread out
so that the air between shone
as it narrowed, stretched, shivered.

A bird, never catching its breath,
sang invisibly, not hidden
yet not to be seen by me,

and from the gravel by my foot
a darker-than-red, a crimson
poppy swayed on a thin stalk.

It seemed we were all – tree
and air and bird and poppy and
gravel even – composing together

a secret no one of us
could know, not one escape.
Which breathes itself in us.

Joan Condon

For Adults Only

Do you think that a woman's task in life
is to hold a man's trousers up?
zoom, let's snuggle sideways;
I feel rhythmic, sudden, primeval.

If only one could write a poem
with no lines, only spaces;

but your heart is closed
like a post office on Sundays;
or perhaps you're for adults only?

Let's talk of computers among the roses
and winged serpents.

We were happy somewhere else
in another garden, long ago;
now I taste salt, I dream of falling
through glass, at the edge of electricity;

here are lasers, terrors, paradoxes.

Kay Cotton

Prayer for a tank stuck in mud

Oh Goddess of the Autumn weather
let it rain, let it pour.
We'll climb out of this body,
we'll dance. We'll stamp our feet,
raise the sound of thunder
from this broken beast, this empty drum.

Let it sink into the winter mud.
We'll store grain in its belly, spill
libations from its turrets for the souls
of those who made it, sold it, bought it,
make a flute of its long nose,
a song to sing on Solstice night.

We'll invite the god of fire to burn
the logs wedged in its tracks
and feast on fat eels found beneath.
We'll make light from its oil,
write paeans to peace, long letters
to Amnesty International.

And in the Spring, we'll hole it, carefully,
fill it with blessings of dung, bury it
in soil washed down from the mountains,
grow sweet potatoes, plant trees in its head –
an apple and a peach, a plum and a pear
to bear the fruits of war.

Margaret Crompton

Occupational therapy 1879

Emily sends me wool to knit
blankets and scarves and cheerful words
      as if stitches
and plain and purl could soothe distress
re-ravel my wits.
      Click click
      *Lu*natic
Confess   plain   sin
Yes pure purl cast off.   Forgive
      Click lunatic click-atic
my unbelief,
Lord, want of love, grief,
temptation casts me out. Clickating
needles vex my head with
pain knitting
brings no relief

I am very very desolate

Emily Tennyson and Louisa Turner were sisters and, as wives of the poet brothers Alfred Tennyson and Charles Turner, also sisters- in-law. Emily sent loving letters, and wool to knit blankets and scarves, during Louisa's last weeks of life, in a lunatic asylum. This poem uses words which Louisa often wrote in her almost illegible diaries and other fragments: 'distress, confess, sin, forgive, unbelief, want of love, grief, temptation, vex, pain,' *and the last line –* 'I am very very desolate'.

Peter Daniels

Being English

Farmers of Heathrow, my mother's family were Anglo-Saxon,
but for one Scottish great-grandmother to leaven the English.

My Jewish father, raised and schooled in Edinburgh,
left Scotland and Judaism. Did that make him English?

Hitler would think me Jewish enough, the Chief Rabbi
(should I ask him) wouldn't: default position – English.

I grew up in suburban Birmingham, my mixed blood
mingled with the soft Welsh water stolen by the English.

My language was delivered to me with the bottled milk
at the doorstep and at school. My greatest gift, my English.

By this blessing I'm entitled to take it all for granted,
and mutter under my breath at this land of the English.

Forgetfully arrogant, trying not to try too hard, proudly
we take up the cringe: pardon our empire, we're English.

Understatement and gentle irony, you say, have sunk us
underneath fair play and self-blame. We can be just "too
English."

I'm afraid so – though, while you're saying it, the ones
who like to be disliked will be counting up who counts as
English.

Bury me elsewhere if you must, but I can claim the earth
beneath Terminal 3: a place to welcome you in English.

Out There

where there is
whatever there is,
pushing through arching brambles, tall grass,
whatever's next, I meet
somebody coming the other way,
meeting me instead of
the unmet next step and the next step
– and we stop, we share our reasons
for not being indoors just now:
the sky and the river, but
also the thing inside.

And we treat what's wrong with a life
with whatever we've got: these open marshes,
late evening at the turn of the summer.
We talk about our conditions a little,
shake hands and move our opposite ways,
mirroring each other's
embrace of whatever else
comes next, the overgrowing towpath,
cow parsley heading up, docks
in their rusty towers,
the passing zoom of juicy insects,
and spiders free from their webs
floating out there on paid-out lines of silk.

Julia Darling 1956-2005

End

Eventually, I was placed on a bed like a boat
in an empty room with sky filled windows,
with azure blue pillows, the leopard-like quilt.

It was English tea time, with the kind of light
that electrifies the ordinary. It had just stopped raining.
Beads of water on glass glittered like secrets.

In another room they were baking, mulling wine.
I was warm with cloves, melting butter, demerara,
and wearing your pyjamas. My felt slippers

waited on the floor. Then the door opened
soundlessly, and I climbed out of bed.
It was like slipping on to the back of a horse,

and the room folded in, like a pop up story
then the house, and the Vale. Even the songs
and prayers tidied themselves into grooves

and the impossible hospital laid down its chimneys
its sluices, tired doctors, and waiting room chairs.
And I came here.   It was easy to leave.

Apology for absence

Look, it's as if my heart is a damp cupboard
filled with old brass that needs polishing.

Or I must cover myself with moss, damp down,
try to establish new growth in the rotting.

Sometimes I am whipped to shreds by the North wind
and must curl up beneath a counterpane.

I need to practise dying, imagine health,
to eat tinned pears, light unnecessary fires.

And love can be tyrannical, so sweet, yet edgy.
I am almost overpowered by its fragrant red roses.

Sitting rooms are too vivid. Things get torn.
I have to disappear, to darn each rip.

Forgive me, brave daughters, for the questions
that I have failed to answer. And my love,

Please don't say I malingered, don't be
angry later, when you add up the ticks.

Anna Dear

View from Tregear
(for Barbara Prys-Williams)

One by one they've been switching on the lights,
their warm eyes shining in the brick face over there.
And mine for them, I trust, from over here.

I write; time passes. The window is a mirror now.
I catch myself, watching, working on and lit
by bulbs of light made distantly by others.

I see the bright September apples slip
into the shadows of their leaves and disappear.
I feel the weight,

the freight, of every word, of
apple, tree and light; the night that's falling,
dusky…

a two-way word that brings across the border
two ways of making meaning: you learn, you teach;
you teach, you learn.

Under the trees the windfalls wait, unseen.
I'll walk back into company tonight
with their sweet fermentation in the air.

Woodbrooke, September 2011

dysgu *(pronounced 'dusky') is Welsh for both 'to teach' and 'to learn'*

Ann Drysdale

Dogs in the Wind

Facing four-square into the roaring West,
The little mongrel bravely stands his ground
Among the tempest-tattered meadow-grass.
His hair combed back by the wind's strong fingers,
He holds tight to the earth with spiny feet
As panic-stricken things go whirling past,
Riding on yellow leaves.

Hearing another unfamiliar sound,
Like the dull thrumming of a happy heart,
He turns, tickled by curiosity.
The wind has blown the dust off a lost cause
And the old lurcher, high on borrowed time,
Ears thin as string, mouth wide, cheeks wuthering,
Remembers how to fly.

Migrant Workers

They arrived under cover of darkness.
I saw them when I went out in the morning
To call the gimmers down into the intake.
Their wooden shacks are parked in groups of four
Under the shelter of the old stone wall.

Their open doors face north, south, east and west
And forth they come, humming the usual tune
As sunshine burnishes their uniforms
And warms them as they rise, a living stream
Pouring over the wall on to the heather.

They turn up every year, the migrant workers,
Brought in from further south to carry out
The task set by their masters. Giddy gangs,
Sucking the best out of the fragrant crop.
Seasonal visitors, bringing the harvest home.

U A Fanthorpe 1929-2009

Collateral Damage

The minor diplomat who brings terms for a ceasefire
Enters through a side-door, in the small hours,
Wearing a belted raincoat.

The children have become bold. At the first siren
They cried, and ran for their mothers.
Now they are worldly-wise,

They clamour to watch dogfights above the house,
They prefer under-the-kitchen-table to the shelter,
They play fighting games

Of reading the paper by bomblight,
Pretending to be the enemy. These children
Are no longer safe.

They have learned rash and contrary for ever. Come soon,
O minor diplomat in the belted raincoat, come
To capitulate. For the children have ack-ack nerves,
And a landmine has fallen next door.

Under the reservoir, under the wind-figured water,
Are the walls, the church, the houses,
The small human things,

That in drought rise up gaunt and dripping,
And it was once Mardale, both is and is not Mardale,
but is still there,

Like the diplomat, and the crazy fearless children
Who progress through their proper stages, and the churchbells
With their nightly riddles,

And the diplomat, and the children still running
Away from shelter, into the path of the bomb.

Afterwards

The principalities, the powers, the politicians,
The ones who pose in the spotlight
Centre-stage, and magnetise us as they stalk
Towards bankruptcy, murder, betrayal, suicide
And other traditional exits.

The audience leaves, discussing nuances.
A scatter of sweet-papers, ash,
Smells hanging around behind. The audience leaves.

And in they come, rolling up their sleeves,
With hoovers and mops, buckets and brushes and Brasso,
Making it ready for the next time, nobody watching,
With small uncompetitive jokes, with backchat
About coach-trips, soaps, old men,
And a great sloshing of water.

This is where we ought to be. Not
Up on the stage with the rich and the Richards,
Rehearsing already their entry for the next house,
The precise strut that registers power,

But down on our hands and knees,
Laughing, and mopping up.

Rising Damp
(for C.A.K. and R.K.M.)

'A river can sometimes be diverted, but it is a very hard thing to lose it altogether.'
> *(J G Head: paper read to the Auctioneers' Institute in 1907)*

At our feet they lie low,
The little fervent underground
Rivers of London

Effra, Graveney, Falcon, Quaggy,
Wandle, Walbrook, Tyburn, Fleet

Whose names are disfigured,
Frayed, effaced.

These are the Magogs that chewed the clay
To the basin that London nestles in.
These are the currents that chiselled the city,
That washed the clothes and turned the mills,
Where children drank and salmon swam
And wells were holy.

They have gone under.
Boxed, like the magician's assistant.
Buried alive in earth.
Forgotten, like the dead.

They return spectrally after heavy rain,
Confounding suburban gardens. They infiltrate
Chronic bronchitis statistics. A silken
Slur haunts dwellings by shrouded
Watercourses, and is taken
For the footing of the dead.

Being of our world, they will return
(Westbourne, caged at Sloane Square,
Will jack from his box),
Will deluge cellars, detonate manholes,
Plant effluent on our faces,
Sink the city.

Effra,Graveney, Falcon, Quaggy,
Wandle, Walbrook, Tyburn, Fleet

It is the other rivers that lie
Lower, that touch us only in dreams
That never surface. We feel their tug
As a dowser's rod bends to the source below

Phlegethon, Acheron, Lethe, Styx.

Sue Flemons

Journey's End

They reached a terminus
And properly interred
Thought to await eternity
Undisturbed.

Prosaic progress
Grubbed up their bones;
It was poetry perhaps
Lifted their stones,

Stacked them in circles
Among the ash tree roots....

Now weathered, wordless,
Woven with bramble shoots,

They seem an outcrop
Of the aeons beneath,
Impersonal, impassive
As boulders on Egdon Heath.

*As a young architect, Thomas Hardy was responsible for clearing part
of Old St Pancras churchyard to make way for the London Midland
Railway. The headstones were arranged around a tree, where they can
still be seen.*

Kate Foley

Tikkun Olam
Mending the World

Season of jars and bottles when foetal plums
curl in on themselves, a bloodknot, rich on kitchen shelves,

when apples blaze like emperors,
when there are leaves on the line.

Though the cropped lion's ruff in fields
suggests a yield that never came,

because the Crack of Doom's so slow,
you can forget the scruffy bees

that rub their balding bodies
on scanty pollen while pigeons inch

on crippled feet.
You'd rather sweep out on a clean tsunami

with blackened fag-end flies, stained plastic,
disembowelled tvs

but now the virtual plastic of the Stock Exchange
in domino effect means Footsie's fall's

the only wave you'll get. Season of fruit
whose colours lend decay

romance, the world's wound stinks
like a bird in the chimney.

Mending is no hero's task. Think
instead, raw threads, cobbled patches,

tear-stained, blood-stained needle pricks
and where its rotten fabric parts

a patient, industrious makeover
of the heart.

In Quaker Meeting

When he wakes
        to find himself in the transparent air of meeting
the old man's smile reflects the inverse curve of his painful back.
        Old women sit, their hands like root vegetables.
Their laps are at peace.
        Surely we all have the same secrets
locked between our thighs, the same shabby bald spots
        on the nap of love or action?

Goodness rises like cream, skimmed by the light.
        Give me some of that I want to say
but there is no-one to ask and only
        the plain light from the windows,
the small scrunch and shift
        of elderly bones on a bench.

Annie Foster

Cold morning

I do not visit your grave
on the slope above the Caldew
but I am not far off

the broad sky pulls up
a pillar of factory smoke;
smoke by day, fire by night

sun lifts steam from the broken flow
and a mallard flies the river path,
its tail a tight curl

I kick and kick at mole heaps
some, frozen, bounce my foot
some give

frost has formed flood debris
into glittering noodles;
I disturb the heron

on standing water, ice spokes;
every grasshead in the meadow
flowering white

when her world unravelled
she filled her pockets with stones
and walked into the Ouse

I will not, though death has
cancelled my last chance of you
and joy is unhinged

this winter morning
where the water runs smooth
there is calm.

Eternal

Open the thin skin of glass
let seals call into your dream.
Sea up, you walk to the island
slowly, water is thicker than air.
Sea down, you crunch over mussels,
stroke the air from matted hair,
soft green weed, sunwarmed.

Wallflowers on old walls smell hazy yellow,
among pale tufts of thrift,
wild stunted thyme on your fingers.
See the bees, ecstatic, wind in the poppy's orange pistil.

Tide up, look inland to the larks,
tufted heads are rising,
rising from field to infinity,
heron lifts his path over water,
goldfinches tease in hedgerows,
bosomy sparrows come close,
tap their beaks on the trellis.

Tide down, the seabirds feed;
oyster-catcher scimitars,
black white red,
formation flying round the rock circle.
Plover's bead eye watching
godwit and curlew; beaks up
beaks down, press into the sand.

Open the thin skin of glass
let the wave sound, birdsong, seal song
enter your dream and let yourself
bleed out into the eternal.

Andrew Greaves

Lost Children

so in this dream
I'm toiling away
in blistering heat
on a hillside in Palestine
ploughing stony soil
with the jaw-bone of an ass
it's damned hard work
what with all the armed men
that keep leaping up out of the furrows
and the nasty little fragments of live scripture
this earth's infested with
they can blow up any time
causing heavy loss of life
I'm standing on the hillside gazing round
and in all directions
far as eye can see
the phosphorescent glare
of flash new settlements
well cities built on hill-tops can't be hid
the Judean desert's all but gone
rough places straightened
the valley lifted up
exactly as promised
a six-lane highway scrawled across the plain
in the wilderness that's left behind
I wake up to the sound of many voices crying

Philip Gross

The Quakers of Pompeii
Quaker Meeting (sculpture), Peter Peri

Let's say the ash came down;
        we were forged and preserved.
Here's a good girl, sitting up at table
        waiting to be served.

This woman's big hands
        think nappies, think bleach.
She'll give the world a clip around the earhole
        if it gets within reach.

That man is hugging
        something spiky to his heart.
This one says *Sorry, Sir* (though he's a big
        boy now) *it fell apart*

in my hands. Age
        tenses this one like a spring
or a grasshopper, poised to flick away
        into nothing. Or to sing.

This one's a sit-down striker
        who Will Not Be Moved.
That handcuffed convict waits
        for his appeal to be refused

again, again. This woman stays
        slumped backwards where
somebody knocked her. She hides her face.
        She holds the chair.

The last man frankly
         wants to be excused…
as well we all might if the final flash-
         bulb caught our attitudes,

when the clay we've been moulding
         eventually bakes.
Until then, listen to them breathing. Love
         the fidgets. Love the aches.

from **Vocable**

14.

About the sacredness of breath they were not wrong,
the Hebrew masters — scribes
who hinted at the vowel sounds
in jots and tittles

like the name of YHWH
like the breath of Him

easing between our sticks, stones,
mud bricks, consonants and laws, those dry
bones (otherwise, how could they live?),
between our definitions

and not one, not all
the languages of earth

can hold it, that without
which the most hallowed rank of script
becomes calligraphised barbed wire,
a wall.

Retreat

Stepped aside from our separate lives
together, in the garden, we are not alone –
St Francis skulking in the laurels, and a hack,
pause, pant, hack: Father Cormac coming through

with a billhook, in shirtsleeves. It's all he can do,
he says, to keep the paths open, not to mention
the rabbits that crater the thin grass
like a small bombardment night by night.

If he had his way, he'd pave it all,
the lawn around the grotto. Lourdes
in local fluted limestone, it has Bernadette
on her knees while, a statue adored

by a statue, Mary lifts her pale blue
slightly crumbling plaster eyes.
A smudge of mould muddies her hem
as if she'd got down to it, taking her turn

trampling wild garlic and bluebell stalks
crisp as asparagus, or raking out the pond
whose plaster heron tilts askew
over embers of goldfish, where the surface

shows as one reflection me and you,
statues, arms to shoulders, arms to waist,
in attitudes of blessed and blessing, that
old miracle. And maybe they'll be kind,

the saints we can't quite credit – not
to make us see, too much, our wildered paths,
our muddied hems, the crumbling plaster
we touch round each other's lips and eyes.

June Hall

Funny Devices

You bet! I could be a midlife dare-devil, do wheelies
with my electric shop-rider, carousels on revolving car seats,
swing from ceiling hoists, sponsor power-chair races.

I'd flick easy-to-open bottle-tops at my open-mouthed children,
seduce my man on satin sheets in shiny pyjamas
designed to help the helpless turn in their adjustable beds;

or I'd whiz up and down on my stair-lift, glowing with giggles,
get drunk in the day from a no-spill mug so full of sherry
that no one would know what sort of tremor I'd got.

Not me. I'll junk this mag with its glossy, know-all face
and pasty backside plastered with aids-for-the-infirm,
heavyweight ads that pack a mean punch.

Not me. I'll shred its pages for paper chase trails,
light bonfires with its two-timing cover, bake potatoes
in its ashes. You won't find me on the ropes for long,

a user of funny devices. Not me. Not yet

Mavis Howard

Translation

He lies in his semi in the dark and thinks of the pygmies.
But he is only a translator.

He thinks of them in the heart of the forests.
Will they get their grant?

Does he even know what they are saying? About the loggers
                                        and miners?
All translators are impartial.

Who interpreted? Who wrote this application? This
                                        recommendation?
Pen-pushers in the high-rise offices

a thousand miles away in Kinshasa? For a price.
Or prices.

Who have never been to the forests.
He lies in the dark.

This fourth-hand language from the time when Leopold
stamped all over

a million-acre back-garden. He thinks of the pygmies.
The loggers and miners.

But he is only a translator. Rated by his NGO for
                                        comprehensibility.
And he is impartial.

Susanne Knowles 1911-?

Fox Dancing

Tall as a foxglove spire, on tiptoe
The fox in the wilderness dances;
His pelt and burnished claws reflect
The sun's and the moon's glances.

From blackberry nose to pride of tail
He is elegant, he is gay;
With his pawsteps as a pattern of joy
He transfigures the day.

For a hat he wears a rhubarb leaf
To keep his thinking cool,
Through which his fur-lined ears prick up.
This fox, he is no fool

And does not give a good-morning
For the condition of his soul;
With the fox dancing in the desert
Study to be whole.

Stevie Krayer

Sunbrick Burial Ground

A ewe with her lamb, that fled
as we came in, hovers at the entrance
scratching her backside on the jamb
as she waits for us to leave.

Not that the grass in here is any richer
for the dust beneath. After all those centuries
there can't be much virtue remaining
from two hundred buried Quakers.

A straggle of trees round the boundary
form the honour guard: one nipped hawthorn
holding back its blossom, a half-dozen
unsentimental ash like old soldiers

brutally barbered by the wind,
easing tired backs out of the rock, dangling
fag-ends of bud – and one field maple
flaunting tassels and fluorescent green.

She'd have liked that, old Margaret Fox,
who loved brave colours
and scorned the uniform of Quaker grey –
a silly, poor Gospel:

It's the spirit inside that counts.
She probably wouldn't
have minded that the inscription
chiselled on a boulder

is already half obliterated,
or that some far-off day
all sign of human presence
will have been wiped.

So we walk up to the trig-point, up
into today's May weather and the big clean sky,
above the burial ground and the stone circle
and the Morecambe mud-flats.

High above the golf course and the chemical works,
above the nuclear power station, above
the stark-white wind turbines we take our stand
with larks and limestone and nibbled turf.

*Margaret Fox, the 'mother' of the Quaker movement, is buried at
Sunbrick, on Birkrigg Common in Cumbria*

Nothing but

They say
the sense of awe
can be induced
by stimulating a certain
part of the brain
with an electrode.
So that's awe
shown its place. As if it were nothing
that a feeble buzz of current
can shake open
the many-folded universe
inside 3lb of pink porridge.

Oh, we're ingenious:
our augmented eyes
take us deep into the ocean trenches
of our bodies: pulsing of colonic fins,
branched coral of milk-ducts. We can watch
an ammonite bud into humanity
but it's hammocked
in a life support system
way beyond human contrivance.
What looking-glass mother
will snort at her submariner
Why, you're nothing but a pack of cells!

Some fear knowledge
will gut mystery
like herring, bleed away
its potency. They fear the self-crowned
Lords of Nothing But. But
the real powerhouse
holds nothing
the mind can get a purchase on.
Go march into the Mandelbrot
labyrinth, and when
you've found the end
come back and tell us how you cracked
the walnut of infinity.

John Lampen

Autumn Ghost Festival

The town is suddenly full of spooks, like autumn leaves
silently falling. Last night I saw my grandmother
stand in a queue. The poor thing must be hungry.
She can't lack money, or she wouldn't queue.
Besides I burnt some spirit money for her,
five hundred 'silver squares'. She gave me such
a haunting look — no pun intended. I must put
some nuts and apples on her grave tomorrow.

Ghosts, ghosts, I'm sick of ghosts, behind my back,
under my feet or looking through my window.
I raged to see my aunt — we buried her last year —
in conversation with my gossip neighbour.
What if she tells him how my husband
cheated her of that legacy?
Goodbyes should be goodbyes, I like to say.

As the sun fell, Tian Ming was standing by the woodyard.
I never liked the boy — but still I felt a pang
remembering how he tumbled full of wine
out of a window into darkness. Then Hei Jie
— and nobody had known she liked the boy —
melted away in tears, grew thin and died.
I didn't see her yesterday.

All these transparent faces blowing
about the town like a spilt deck of cards
are part of me — I am what I remember.
But they should hide themselves in decent quiet,
not flap about my ears,
greedy things begging beer and spirit money.
Where have they been that they don't understand
how short things are with us?

Folk tell me that these spooks have pockets
full of good luck to give—but I can tell you
I never saw it left for me to find.

O gods, my little Liu is peeping through the door.
She used to come in here as if she were
my birth-child, play with pebbles on my floor.
Come in, my pet...

                        but she just stands and stares.
If I could throw regrets into the braziers
instead of paper money; if I could make my peace
with these accusing glances; if... if... if...
What can't be cured must be endured, we say.

The Ghost Month in southern China is the seventh lunar month, when the spirits of the dead return to us and have to be placated with gifts of food and specially printed "spirit money" which is burnt on braziers for them.

The fountain of tears

◊

The Khan swore an oath that his beloved girl
should be mourned every moment till the end of days.

So Omar the wise took a pillar of marble
and carved seven bowls where the water falls

from one to the next, a drop at a time—
the Fountain of Tears at Bakhchíserai.

◊ ◊ ◊

I stand where the poet stood and gazed
pondering the nature of chance and love.

As each tear splashes into its basin
it counts another second; imperceptibly

they erode the memory of the much-kissed face
which they were told to preserve for ever.

The subtle engineer and the grieving Khan
fade, as she does, backward into time

leaving me lonely with the drip   drip   drip
of an ageless, nameless ache of loss.

◊

*Bakhchíserai was the capital of the Crimean Tartars from the
fourteenth to the eighteenth century. The Fountain was made about
1756, and Pushkin visited and wrote a poem about it.*

J J Lawson

Lost Country

When the wild geese go over, crying, calling
Into the north wind, heading off to Svalbard,
Drawn out in skeins towards the melting snow,
The paddock geese look up at their lost sky
And wonder, then continue grazing.
The echoing wide of air is gone forever:
Grass is important; grass matters.

The scent of mowing grass, of beans in flower
Comes through the open windows
Of those who scuttle down the concrete roads
That link sad conurbations,
And something for a moment stirs, then dies
As they crowd on to the next junction,
Towards the gym, the supermarket trolley,
Home to the Box and pictures of the hills.
The summer fields have gone below the radar
And left secure the prison of the roads.

Alison Leonard

Callanish Stone Circle

To come here asks nothing
but the shedding of protective turf
and the knowing that for stones to stand
there's one necessity: as much beneath
as is above. And no shoes.

You can greet them,
and in return they will greet you.
Think sinew, breath, retina, bone.
Bring yours, and they will speak with theirs.

Now here's the hardest shedding:
the word 'only'. Only stones.
Naked, without the 'only' judgement,
you can lock eyes with each of them,
and each moment will be a millennium,
and the marrow of your bones will shimmer
as if an orchestra on the most distant star
were playing an ancestral symphony
right by your ear.

For this is where your mother
built her altar, and fashioned it
in awe to face the wind and sun and sea,
not to bow down, but to stand,
shoeless, with her own song,
at the intersection
of the above with the beneath.
She asks of you nothing
but to stand, and let
the bones of your ears pick up the song.

Aphrodite as a Rock

Those old Cypriots who hauled
their thighs aching from the fields
to Aphrodite's sanctuary,
glaring white dust clogged
between their sweating toes
worshipped not a head, a mind,
but a grey-green backboned rock.
It wasn't some frivolity, they
didn't fall in and out of it.
They strove and strained,
stood under the stars,
gave themselves not knowing
what they gave, and often as not
produced only a turd. Or pebble.
Or sweet cyclamen. Or poem. Or child.
No-one predicted what might out-come.
It was what was. The rock said so.

Lawrence Lerner

Residues

My mother, dying, left a wardrobeful,
A world half-worn, half-new:
Old-fashioned underclothes; a row of shoes,
Soles upward, staring; tangles of rings,
Impatient opals, bargain bangles, pearls;
And, flowered or jazzy, rayon, cotton, tulle,
A hundred dresses, waiting.

Left with that ragged past,
My poor truncated father sold the lot.
What could he do? The dealer shrugged, and said,
'Take it or leave it – up to you.' He took
And lost the fiver at the races.
The empty wardrobe stared at him for years.

My father, dying, left a pack of cards,
A presentation clock, a cardboard box
Half-filled with his identity; no books,
No papers. His truncated past
Whisked from my hands, he stepped aside, was gone,
Leaving no litter.

And I, on dying? For my sons, my wife,
My house, my rows of books, my piles of papers,
My mother's letters and my father's clock:
My residue imposing on them all?
Too much, too much.

God's Mothers

'How would you like to wear this cloak?' he asked
– A dark blue taffeta that threw the light
In handfuls at your eyes.
It swished, it tumbled, it caressed. I said,
God made that cloak. I felt the blue, the braid.
But God made everything, he said, and smiled.
– Especially that. Oh most especially that.

I fetched my sister's child. I washed my face,
Put on the cloak, the jewel, the snood of lace,
And let myself be rearranged. He said,
'Love it. Or try to. It's the son of God.'
It pulled my hair. It wet my dress. It cried.
It is the son of Tito Bolognese
And has his shifty eyes. Twisting a hand
Out of my grip, it spilled a pot of paint.
I laughed: 'See what the son of God has done.'

There have been thousands of us, in blue cloaks,
Wearing lace headdresses and holy looks,
Sitting on straw while men in fancy dress
Presented cardboard gifts; baring our breasts
For vanity, or for the love of God,
Or just for money: types of motherhood.
Some with a sister's child, some with their own.
If you're a mother, innocence is gone;
If you're a virgin, where's the mother-love?
It's never right. God watches from above
And lets us play Madonna for an hour,

Or rub our eyes with onions, grow our hair,
And hold a smelly skull, as Magdalen;
Or go and fetch our mother, for St Anne,
God's mother's mother. It was like a game
That's over now: the rest of life is left.

I gave him back his cloak. God's cloak. And wept,
And disappeared into myself again.
And now I hang in the Capella Sancti,
And one day I will be in the Uffizi
– If that is me. God's story is a play,
Which we sit here rehearsing endlessly.
Whether you play the sinner or the saint
Makes little difference. There it is, in paint,
Me as God's mother. Me as penitent.
What in a life is there to single out
Except for that? Oh most especially that.

Alison Lock

Ladybird, Ladybird

I stop the sh sh across my page

to watch a squirrel nuzzle the ground
all auburn fuzz, nose down
re-checking the co-ordinates
on a mental map for a nut called X

the shrubs wear their prettiest bonnets
of permed seed heads, legs
black stockinged from stalking
the late summer rains

the lawn has had its last trim of the year
concentric, whorled
shaved into an Italianate maze.

A four spotted ladybird comes to my sill
I lend her my pen for a bridge
I am curious
now there are six spots
two on the edge of her shell
as if about to fall off, and they do
with a shiver, she splits

into a pair of dash away wings
taking her back to her home.

I carry on with the sh sh across my page.

Robert Maxwell

Ansâri

You, who have made us without charge
And feed us with generosity,
Forgive us with an equally open heart:
You are God who does not act commercially.

I am nothing but a disobedient slave,
So how can you be satisfied with me?
My heart is darkly black: where
Is your light that should be blazing out from me?

But if your grant of paradise depends
On my obeying all your just commands,
That's no more than contractually fair.
Where then's your liberality?

*Translated from the Monâjât, an intimate conversation with the
Divine, written in Persian by Ansâri, who died in 1069 CE.*

Dorothy Nimmo 1933-2001

Christmas Poem

This time of year it gets dark around three –
starts to get dark so you begin to think,
right from the moment you set off, about
the time and how the darkness seems to rise
out of the ground which is so wet, so sodden,
darkness like water rising and flooding the fields
and gathering under the hedgerows, the sky
still pale and the trees (darkness
caught in their wet branches) stand up against it
but the darkness is powerful and you're walking faster
as if you were afraid the darkness
would swallow you up if you stayed out in it,
the water going right over your head
and serve you right, starting out at three
knowing perfectly well the dark was hiding
behind the barn, under the stone wall
and would be there by five. Well you keep going
and by quarter-to you're in the market place
with all the lights blazing and you're safe
until tomorrow when you'll be out again
around three daring it to catch up with you this time.

Homewards

Sheltered from the world's winds, there
under that small tump, bristle-backed,
is the real right place, the epicentre.

Lighthouse to church-spire, standing stone to hill crest,
beacon to beacon along the ley-lines
a sacred webbing stretches across country.

Cat's cradle. Gold threads on her steel needles.
Hear her calling from the secret garden
even from this other summit across the valley.

Demanding only the correct behaviour,
the necessary lie, the polite evasion.
A small gesture would be sufficient.

How hard it is going so far. What tension
walking a different path in another direction.

Black Parrot

Kill the black parrot. Choke the sodding bird,
it never said a kind thing or a true word
or if it did that wasn't what I heard.

I only heard it squawking in my ear
things no-one in their right mind wants to hear
that made me cold with shame and white with fear.

Behave yourself. Control yourself. You know
you don't think that, you only think you do.
You can't just please yourself. I told you so.

You're being selfish. It's for your own good.
You must. You must not. But you know you should.
If you tried harder I am sure you could.

I'm disappointed in you. Never say
I didn't tell you. But you had your way,
you'd not be told. There'll be a price to pay.

Where was it Polly learned that canting word?
It's time to wring its neck, the stupid bird.

What made us think that was the voice of God?

Maggie Norton

Opening the Back Door

This frosty dawn smells of
washing stiffened overnight
in the yard. At once
nothing matters for it arrives
with a remembrance
of somewhere else.

A blackbird cocks his head.
He watches me disappear
on to a towpath
by a hawthorn hedge
where mist whitens the water
and a small wind puffs away night.

One coral dawn like this
I saw a water vole tow
a curtain of lacewing ripples
across the canal.
In my mind I'll swim
after his tracery.

There'll be dew beading the grass
winking diamonds back to fading stars.
A day of flame will stretch out
to the horizon
and take me with it.
This rosy sky is everything.

Christmas on the Lancaster Canal

Creatures of course; rabbits watching
a robin perched on the tiller. Not much
of a show but a presence, like a nip in the air
or frost in a blue sky and a glad rise
of smoke from a wood-burning stove.

Presents of course; a lump of fat
on the hawthorn, peanuts on the towpath
paper cracking off books and boxes
of ginger. The smell of sage and onion
and a crunch of boots before a feast.

Stillness of course; the crack of ice
somewhere else, the little sounds
a landscape utters to listeners
caring for calm. Inside, the chink
of glasses and the smile in your eyes.

Emmaline O'Dowd

Man with concertina
(for Alistair Anderson)

Of course, his fingers command
those past-and-future faces, though
what you mostly see is how it swoops
and circles, would be gone,
if it weren't tethered by his thumbs,
one firm in each leather loop.

It leads him a dance,
as he plays into our eyes, smiling.
But he's not there,
he's in that breathing box
with his inheritance.

Between tunes,
he talks of past masters, fiddlers and pipers,
makes them live again their Tyneside trades,
re-shepherd wide Northumbrian spaces –
friends who gifted him their store.

Now he shares
strand after choice strand,
till the room's festooned with sonic silver,
as if that fat grub,
that procession of stout hexagons,
spun itself a virtual cocoon.

After all, it chooses not to butterfly,
and at the end, amid the whoops and whistles,
sits smug along his arm,
a falcon on a noble's wrist,
every heart hunted, not one escaped.

With Vincent at MoMA*

*"Just as we take the train to get to Tarascon or Rouen, we take death
to reach a star."*

Vincent van Gogh

"Look, this is more than a sower
against a lime-green evening sky.
Look, yes look, there's more here
than stars leaving fingerprints on the midnight river."

You, here in person. Your almost audible voice.

Behind the black figures of the *Stevedores at Arles*
a glory-pouring sunset brimming over the frame.

The real *Starry Night* –
a presence no copy can come near.
I wind myself among its cosmic energies,
a knot so that we'll remember.
You strove with your vision till it blessed you,
and still blesses me, standing to receive your darshan.

Time's up. I hate to go,
To leave you nailed naked to the gallery wall.
I want to comfort you with what I understand:
you saw through seeing
to something beyond. What you came back with
turned your flesh and blood to stars and cypresses.

I step out on to faded pavements,
wander numbered avenues,
know you're still with me
when I see your haloed stars
aswirl with the crescent moon over Liberty Island.

*Museum of Modern Art, New York

Fiona Owen

Christbearer

Who knows what it was about.
Childhood arguments are surely plentiful.

I reached for your St Christopher –
one sharp yank was all it took.
I saw the links of the silver chain
snap, the pendant slipping into your shirt.

I was sorry the other side of the door,
even in that black cloud of fume.

I swam back to you in a sea of tears,
shame smarting my eyes,
and you received me
as an elder might.

Things break so easily – across the years
I've worn this lesson as an amulet.

Mark Pasco

Mall practice

Nobody was honest enough
Nobody was brave enough
To actually declare him mad.
It was a label he might have eaten –
Like he ate the tea-bag, top of the bus,
Going to the hospital.
Mental. The hospital.

His garden was mostly a jacked-up car.
His look, at the door, as
Wild as his upbringing,
Wild as his hair,
Wild as his eyes.

His mother was dead.
His father kept lunacy's legacy marinated –
Drowning his sorrows, he said –
Only his sorrows were strong swimmers.

Luke made me a mug of tea.
He offered toast, but I passed, having passed
The arched arses of several feral cats.

Walking to the shops
Luke herded me,
Wolf-whistled old ladies, nipped at bins,
Dropped his shoulders in a sullen slouch,
Long idle hands in deeply empty pockets.

Writing to the charity had been
The easy part, sitting at my first desk –
Money for clothes to help the teenager look half-
Decent, for Court, for interviews, for goodness sake.

Luke chose garments at speed.

We queued to pay.
Luke wandered off
For belated bursts on
Underwear, belts, a tie, of all things.
When the cash registered
Luke came to heel.
Stood sentinel, a meerkat moment,
Eyes busy translating some chemical equations.
The small body of evidence slid funereally
Towards the cashier.

Luke could not watch. He ducked
Beneath the counter, lay at my feet.
Purchases passed overhead in store-bright bags.
Beneath the counter, beneath the madness, beneath
The motive of my morning
I aimed a playful kick at the foetal boy.
Slightly smiled, mainly to myself.

We had come this far.

Meg Peacocke

An Inventory of Silence

Silence of early, the hour
before birdbreak. Silence hanging

between tick and tock.
A plainsong silence, unmarked stave.

Intima: innermost membrane
thinner than gold leaf: a firmament.

Angle of a thinking head.
The letter not arriving, or having arrived.

A baked clay tablet, clearly incised.
You cannot decipher it.

An electric bulb swinging. Silence
of speaking when you are spoken to,

not finding the words
to say words fail.

Silence, a paraphrase.
A means of making do.

Proposition. A light illicit touch.
Silence like unrisen bread,

blanched knuckles in a row.
Silence in a manner of speaking.

An empty lap. Hands nailed
in the endurance of prayer.

Silence of between, of alone.
At the last, with a bloom to it

And all the stories gathered
like light in one unfallen drop.

Doreen Pearce

Riding a Bicycle Backwards

is a circus trick by clowns
with baggy trousers, thick red lips
and startled eyebrows,
crazy, impossible. Playing for laughs.

Not seeing where you're going,
only where you've been.
Whatever the road brings,
potholes, corners, crossroads,
will take us by surprise,
shake our equilibrium,
change our destinations.

Winifred Rawlins 1907-1997

Man is a Tender Plant

In this our time,
Our sad, new, immeasurably dear time,
Walking at night near the edge, gazing
Down into the abyss, or letting the eyes
Sweep upward, searching out unseen worlds,

It is never enough,
No, never enough now, if you encounter another
Walking the same path, merely to greet him
Carelessly and slip by, eager to begin the descent
To the waiting valley.

Linger with him a moment, ask for news
Of his home, whether he has eaten,
Or knows of a place to rest.

Only yesterday
He grew up in prison in the shadow
Of crematoriums for the living,
Last night lay down to sleep
In a city crumbling to dust around him,
Fled from his home to enter a country
Speaking strange tongues,
Hid behind frail doors
From the night-sticks of despair.

Rachel Rees

One son, predeceased

Technically it was spring
the day they scattered the ashes.

Bin Day. Windy. Dank.

One grey slab of sky
sealed the journey to the end of the land

where she caught the eyes of the relatively few
huddled, umbrellaed on the sand
beyond the carpark.

She wore a mac and a small hat.

The veins in her hands stood blue
rings loose on her fingers.

She read from Romans
she did not break down.

There was a tea later
of the Methodist sort.

Going home
she saw great clumps of daffodils
blown sideways on verges.

Black and scattered down her street
the bins were empty.

She imagined the shouts of the binmen
as she pulled hers in behind her
through to the dark yard.

Marilyn Ricci

Post-Mortem Parenting

Since she died, my mother is a better parent.
Don't get me wrong, she was good. But,
whatever the source of a family row, she
placed herself firmly in its eye, raged at
the rising waters, screamed through cartwheeling air
until we prayed our ears would drop off.

These days she's more down to earth,
strokes my hair when my head's in her lap,
calms the searing fires of doubt,
bites her tongue during any fight,
offers a hug when I wake in the night.
At last, breathes life into my failing heart.

And when you thought

it was long gone, here it is,
up your sleeve, in your pocket,
tucked under a sleeping cat.

You pull it out, let it fall,
drape it over both arms,
admire its improbability

a thin-air hammock, woven in light,
            to be flung up
                        between
a cold house and a home,
harsh words and a smile.

Lie in it. It will hold you.

Joy

knows everything,
on the beach at Rhyl,
pale blue eyes, pretty mouth.

She can build an igloo out of sand,
find a tiny crab like jelly,
not spill a drop from her blue bucket,
dig up the best razor shells.

Joy laughs when she hurts herself,
tells her brother great big lies,
steals from her mother's purse.

All day long I think about living
in an igloo made of sand, cold
damp walls that won't stay solid,
clawing out with sharpened shells.

I like playing with Joy
but all day long
I want to go home.

Mary Rowlands

After the stroke

Why are they so shy
the words he's lost?
If he raises eyes
they bound away
off through deep cloud
unreachable over the hill.

If he sneaks up quietly
keeping his profile low
sometimes he catches one
singly, unaware.

Today came Toaster and Telephone
but, slyly grinning,
Mug and Jug changed places, saying
they would not be owned.

He struggles to catch them.
They are wild things, words.
They deny him rights,
coming neither to whistle nor cry,

but, when he looks away,
bending heads to halter
gently they lick his hands
unmastered still
yet, as before, his friends.

Carol Rowntree Jones

Sensuous, there was nothing sensuous

It was a shop that sold loose vinegar.
Cheddar triangulated with a wire.
The lime washed cellar where a side of bacon hung.
Muslin wrapped cheeses brewing their rank tang.

Loose raisins, currants, cherries.
Sticky and stuck together in square corners.
Square blocks in plastic lined boxes.
Tamped down quarter pound cellophane bags.

The boning of the bacon. County cricket. Larks.
Two knife flicks, one each side of the rib.
Knotted string, pulled sharp to rip the rib
clean to throw the smoked, or plain, cage unribbed
with a dull fat thud where it is sliced exactly
thick or near transparent thinness. Cow parsley.

Sibyl Ruth

Chapel, Women's Hospital

When you left the two of us
on that first day

the child breathed at my side
in her clear box.
A new work on display.

Before driving home
you walked along a corridor
into a plain room

where dry flowers bloomed in a vase.
Just a few rows of chairs,
a book in a glass case
with a list of names.

Many more than you could hold or touch.

The record of those
whose boxes had been put away
sealed up.

And you knew we had done nothing.
Nothing to deserve
the size, the shape, the sheer weight of our luck.

Blood rang in your ears.
Your neck grew tight.
Words couldn't be enough.

But prayer surged at your throat.
It cried out. And you said
Thanks.

Thank you very much.

Clive Sansom 1910-1981

The Timeless Hour

Let action go; and with it all the thought
Of action. Even when the world is racked,
It may be worthier to refrain from action
Than it is to act.

Forget the world one hour; when you return
Its beauty will be there, its tragedy;
And though the past and future shake their chains,
The now is free.

Think yourself out of thinking; exorcise
Even that ghost of thought, the echoing word –
Till in the haunted chamber of the brain
No sound is heard.

Then, when its windows open on a world
Beyond the world, when all its walls are dumb,
Into the silent room, the wordless mind,
The Word may come.

Brigid Sivill

Today they bury you and I am far away

up to Phundar in the night,
rocky edges pressing the road.
I know because I read it
we are climbing high
but the dark refuses a horizon.
On a wide corner the jeep slows
I hear water spilling down the mountainside.
I know it is blue (see above)
extraordinary tropic blue.
Blueness splashing from rock to rock.

They have gone
the sad procession of the dead
who no longer wake to the bite
of morning mountains
remaining only a drift of ash turning in the wind.

This long journey, dust sealing up the eyes,
ends on a sudden lip of land.
A light hangs in the dark,
not a night beacon but a shower of brightness;
a small lake and a surround of peaks.
Over all, a bowl of stars
crowding the sky,
bringing it down
spiral by spiral
to the rope of land.

The island where I fetched up

On my small island
stitched a life
sustained by water, wind and sky.
Wood, tarred barrel,
linen sail, a broken spar,
I gathered up.

The perfect shell
slipped easily
between my fingers.
Sometimes I bathed.
The curling sea
wrapped me in its glassy arms.

I was not afraid to enter.
I was no longer wrecked.
The gaps between waves sang to me,
birds threaded the trees
with the sound of it;
inside the song I grew.

Light blessed me.
I was washed by it.
Laid out, perfectly,
I waited
resurrection.

Mosedale Meeting House

Mosedale.
The pinch of dusty air
with its granite wall
enclosing the reach of fell.

Barn End. Where a red fox
paused, mid jump,
the limp duck
hanging from his mouth.

Carrock Fell.
Round, unfettered hills
where a sudden cloudburst
took the path in a gush of water.

The stone pen,
where the silent shepherd
placed his dog
while he waited for the light.

Grey cloth and bridled tongue.
The hat placed, just so, upon a wooden peg
before the elder shook God's words
out of his mouth.

Here is stone enclosing stillness.
Feel, in the bitter cold,
standing in Carrock light,
the soul stripping to its bone.

Ruth Terrington

Storing Apples

The apples have had a good year,
better than mine. They hardly need
validation such as my rough
words bestow. Harvested

they have the final say; their glut
makes me a fool. I sit and sort
and wrap and stack, my hands a mess
of juice and newsprint. Storing them

on wooden trays, I wager I'll behold
their restoration: that's the trick
I've found elusive. After rain
of February, opening the shed

that's warped with cold and wet, I smell
the mix of sound and rotted fruit
and count my luck. A touch discerns
those that outlasted firm and sweet

the frost, and those now friable
inside their wrinkled cerements, or turned
to pulp, their failure palpable.
Some act of violence, I think,

must resurrect them, hurling stones
and earth aside. Or could one word
change everything, as quietly
as north reverts to south, unrecognised?

The Bird-bit

Pastry's a knack that comes from making do
in the lean years. My mother had that deft
economy, seizing on every curl
from the pie's rim. She'd learned her thrift

from girlhood. (*Her* mother would slice ham
nearer the bone than Truth; would spread
butter like gold-leaf!) But after all was done
another imperative remained, unsaid:

from the floured board she'd pinch and pull
the pallid scraps together, shaping them
into the rough knob she used to call
the bird-bit. Solemnly we'd put it to bake

alongside the proper food. When it was done
we'd throw it, warm, on to the grass and watch
the starlings squabble over it. No-one
bothered to spell it out: simply, for each

harvest we knew some leeway must remain,
an untouched margin. This was the true
thrift, leaving a mite for those to glean
who in *your* want would do the same for you.

Bob Ward

Fables

Mist encloses overhead
  as a honking riot
  flocks through invisibly.
They're Gabble Ratchets,
  Gabriel's Hounds, or souls
  rent from dead children
  un-baptized; in callous lore
  consigned to restlessness
  until some Judgment Day.
Would that one of ours
  be crying out among them,
  that mite-let who miscarried
  while not yet personable,
  too unformed for grief?
Forty years pass in mist;
  now suddenly I find
  my self repossessed
  by this need for prayer:
  that our one wandering
  spirit-child, goose-footed,
  may go to graze for ever
  across the Elysian Fields,
  were they to exist.

Clare Wigzell

Benediction
After Carol Ann Duffy's poem 'Premonition'

Words ice up the windscreen.
Door smacks; your long limbs follow
To your girlfriend's door. It's twilight.
I don't know you any more. The last
Birds finish their song. I shudder.
The darkness closes in around me.

We drive backwards together.
Your sharp retorts are sucked back,
My questions, too direct for you,
Dissolve into hesitant air.
Our shoulders give, heart rates slow.
The late sun shines more strongly.

Summer returns. Your bedroom door
Unlocks, is left ajar, swings open.
You leave your friends to seek me out.
One evening, as I lift your brother
From the bath, your eyes hook mine,
We rhyme home-work couplets in steam.

The days start when you shout my name.
Shorter and curlier, you flicker like
Dappled light. First night away,
The page is blank; when you run to me
The pencil falls; we sit, breathe,
Feel each other's heart beat.

I suckle you on my folds of fat.
You pull at the milk ducts, eyes
Wide open, drinking me. In
The grey before dawn, I give up
Being at the centre of my life.
My womb already misses you.

Waldo Williams 1904-1971

Translations by Stevie Krayer

Pa beth yw dyn?

Beth yw byw? Cael neuadd fawr
Rhwng cyfyng furiau.
Beth yw adnabod? Cael un gwraidd
Dan y canghennau.

Beth yw credu? Gwarchod tref
Nes dyfod derbyn.
Beth yw maddau? Cael ffordd trwy'r drain
At ochr hen elyn.

Beth yw canu? Cael o'r creu
Ei hen athrylith.
Beth yw gweithio ond gwneud cân
O'r coed a'r gwenith?

Beth yw trefnu teyrnas? Crefft
Sydd eto'n cropian.
A'i harfogi? Rhoi'r cyllyll
Yn llaw'r baban.

Beth yw bod yn genedl? Dawn
Yn nwfn galon.
Beth yw gwladgarwch? Cadw tŷ
Mewn cwmwl tystion.

Beth yw'r byd i'r nerthol mawr?
Cylch yn treiglo.
Beth yw'r byd i blant y llawr?
Crud yn siglo.

What is Man?

What is living? A great hall
Between narrow walls.
What is knowing? One root
Beneath all the branches.

What is believing? Holding out
Until relief comes.
And forgiving? A path through thorns
To the side of an old enemy.

What is singing? Regaining
Creation's old genius.
And what is work but a song
Made from the wood and the wheat?

What is statecraft? A skill
Still crawling.
And defence of the realm?
Putting a knife in a baby's hand.

What is it to be a people? A gift
In the depths of the heart.
And love of country? Keeping house
In a cloud of witnesses.

What is the world to the great powers?
A circle turning.
And to the children of the lowly?
A cradle rocking.

Medi

Uchel yw pren y bydoedd
A Medi ydyw'r mis
Y plyg yr haul mawr aeddfed
Ei ystwyth gainc yn is.

A than ei thrymlwyth hithau
Mae cainc o'r pren sy'n hŷn
Yn gwyro trwy'r llonyddwch
I lawr at galon dyn.

A rhwng tymhorau daear
Ymrithia amgen wedd.
Ynghanol oesol rhyfel
Mihangel y mae hedd.

Harvest

The tree of the worlds is tall
But September is the season
When the full-grown harvest sun
Makes the yielding boughs sink down.

And under the heavy weight
The boughs of an older tree
Sink lower, through the quiet
Down to the human heart.

And in between earth's seasons
It assumes a different face.
In the thick of the incessant
war of heaven, there is peace.

Medi, *the Welsh word for harvest, also means September.*

119

Emily Wills

Football for Girls

All over England's green and recreation grounds
they're rallying, in arbitrary sponsored shirts,
drawstring shorts flapping on prepubescent knees.

Here are dads in embarrassing sunhats or full kit
and bulbous calves, yelling at the ref, at Lucy,
Hattie, Clare, as they pass and shoot through growing pains,

the chafe of breast buds, sweat rinsing their newly pierced
ears.
There goes Astrid, wobbling inconvenient hips; here's Lou
still knobbly as a twig, winging it end to end.

Sidelined, imaginary, the grans, the greats, tattle and peer
hobbled in ankle skirts, their handspan waists pulled tight,
buttoned, bodiced, pale with parasols. They'd be shouting too

if they could summon up the breath. And my mother,
red faced still
from the fifties staffroom whispering – *my dear,*
she was seen in the garden
wearing trousers.

Biographical notes

Jo Alberti is a retired historian, now engaged in campaigning for a world where Quaker values would have more space to thrive. She writes short plays to this purpose.

Gillian Allnutt lives near Durham. In 2005 she won the Northern Rock Foundation Writer's Award. Her eighth collection, *indwelling*, is due to be published by Bloodaxe Books in September 2013.

Angela Arnold has written poetry all her life. She is also an artist, has published two books on psychological-astrology and has worked as a creative gardener.

Bryan Aspden (1933-1999) published two books of poetry and numerous poems in journals. He lived in North Wales from 1963 and was a member of Colwyn Bay Quaker Meeting.

Elizabeth Bailey began writing poems in a 1989 Gifts and Discoveries [Quaker study pack] group at Central Manchester Meeting. They are far and few now, given time spent with family, asylum seekers, stonecarvers and Oxfam.

R V Bailey has published five collections of poetry, including one with her late life-partner U A Fanthorpe.

Jennifer Barraclough. Roots and most adult life in Yorkshire. Completed working life in 2010 as Director of Woodbrooke Quaker Study Centre.

Jackie Bartlett. Jackie's writing includes short stories, essays and journaling as well as poetry. She has been a Quaker for 25 years and is a member of Thaxted Area Quaker Meeting.

Alice Beer (1912-2011). Orthodox Jewish, pacifist and socialist, Alice left Vienna for England in the 1930s. Later she became a devoted Quaker, and also found time to concentrate on pottery and poetry. An Arvon course taught by U A Fanthorpe encouraged her to publish *Facing Forward Looking Back* (2000); two more successful collections followed.

Kathleen Bell has been a Quaker for nearly 30 years. She teaches Creative Writing and English at De Montfort University and has published poetry, fiction and criticism.

Peter Bennet has published six books of poetry and several pamphlets. He was shortlisted for the T.S. Eliot Prize in 2008. His seventh collection, *Border*, is due from Bloodaxe.

Catherine Benson is a Yorkshire Quaker. She is published in many anthologies. She has two collections, *It Must Have Been a Sunday* and, most recently, *Untitled as Yet*, both published by Smith/Doorstop.

Gerard Benson is a much anthologised poet, who has had nine collections. He was a leading member of the Barrow Poets and is one of the trio which runs Poems on the Underground.

David Blamires is a life-long Quaker and a former editor of *The Friends Quarterly*. Before retirement he taught medieval German and children's literature at Manchester University. He collects alphabet books and has organized exhibitions on Robin Hood, the Book of Jonah and Grimms' fairytales at various Manchester libraries.

Basil Bunting (1900-1985). Northumbrian poet and pacifist (imprisoned in 1918), Bunting was a friend of Ezra Pound, and the full version of his long poem 'Briggflatts' has come to be recognised as one of the key texts of British modernism. He listed as major influences 'Jails and the sea, Quaker mysticism and socialist politics...'

Robbie Burton lives in North Wales and is an attender at Chester meeting. Her poems have been published widely in magazines and anthologies.

Helena Chambers began writing poetry in her fifties, and is encouraged to be included in this volume. She is employed by Quaker Action on Alcohol and Drugs.

Jenny Chantler is a member of Bury St Edmunds Quaker Meeting, 'having stumbled there from an Anglican initiation, a student empathy for Zen Buddhism and a place with nothing at all'. Received a Commended Prize from The Society of Women Writers and Journalists. Member of Bury Poetry Aloud and Suffolk Poetry Society.

Anne Cluysenaar's *Timeslips* (Carcanet) includes 'Vaughan Variations'. Other collections: *Batu-Angas: Envisioning Nature with Alfred Russel Wallace* (Seren), *Water to Breath* (Flarestack),

Migrations (Cinnamon), *From Seen to Unseen and Back* (due Cinnamon, 2014).

Joan Condon is 80 and a member of Selly Oak Quaker Meeting. She has won lots of awards for poetry and has been nominated as Birmingham's poet laureate. *For Adults Only* won second prize in the Yorkshire Open Poetry Competition in 2009.

Kay Cotton. Formerly of Portsmouth Quaker Meeting, Kay now lives in Normandy, where she and her partner offer poetry and music courses and retreats. She loves writing, cooking, family and friends.

Margaret Crompton (Lincolnshire Area Quaker Meeting), a Quaker since 1978, writes and teaches about children's spiritual wellbeing, reviews books for *Friends Journal (Philadelphia)* and, with her husband, John, lectures on English literature.

Peter Daniels has twice won the Poetry Business pamphlet competition (1991 and 1999), and came first in the 2002 Ledbury, 2008 Arvon, and 2010 TLS poetry competitions. His first full poetry collection is *Counting Eggs* from Mulfran Press (2012). His translations of Vladislav Khodasevich from Russian will be published by Angel Classics in autumn 2013.

Julia Darling (1956-2005) began her career as a poet working with performance group The Poetry Virgins, 'taking poetry to the places that least expected it'. As well as her two distinguished collections of poems, *Sudden Collapses in Public Places* (2003) and *Apology for absence* (2004), she wrote short stories and two very successful novels; she also worked on arts and health projects.

Anna Dear was born and brought up in Monmouthshire. Before retiring she taught English and Drama in South Wales and in the Midlands and has run writing workshops for the National Extension College.

Ann Drysdale has published five poetry collections, as well as memoir, essays and a gonzo guidebook to the City of Newport. She lives in a mining town in South Wales.

U A Fanthorpe (1929-2009) taught for sixteen years before abandoning a respectable salary to work as a hospital clerk in Bristol – an experience which pitchforked her into poetry. She published nine poetry collections, as well as *New and Collected Poems* (2003). CBE and FRSL, she was awarded The Queen's Gold Medal for Poetry in 2003.

Sue Flemons Born 1939. Studied and worked in London (teaching and social work). Married painter John Flemons. Four children, nine grandchildren. Quaker since 1980s. Latterly Quaker Prison Chaplin at Wormwood Scrubs. Interests: People, nature, arts.

Kate Foley lives between Amsterdam and Suffolk. Both the chapbook, *A Fox Assisted Cure* and her fifth full collection, *One Window North*, were published by Shoestring Press in 2012.

Annie Foster is a member of Carlisle Quaker Meeting. She has written for forty years and is unlikely to stop. She writes about the relationship between the outer and inner worlds. She has had work published in Bloodaxe *The New Lake Poets* and *Flambard New Poets: No 1* as well as many anthologies.

Andrew Greaves. A member of Hexham Quaker Meeting in Northumberland. Retired teacher of English. A co-founder of The Quaker Community, Bamford, 1988. Since 2009, active supporter of The Villages Group, an Israeli/Palestinian network involved in development and community-building projects in the Occupied West Bank.

Philip Gross is a writer for adults and children, Professor of Creative Writing at Glamorgan University and a member of Penarth Meeting. He has published twenty collections of poetry, including *The Water Table,* which won the TS Eliot Prize 2009, and ten novels for young people.

June Hall has published two collections, *The Now of Snow* and *Bowing to Winter* (Belgrave Press 2004, 2010). Now working on a third, plus a contemporary poetry anthology with R.V.Bailey about loss.

Mavis Howard has been a member of Oxford Quaker Meeting for about forty years. She writes poetry and plays. She sometimes dreams of writing the 'perfect' sonnet – whatever that might mean.

Susanne Knowles (1911- ?) published four collections of poetry plus two anthologies between 1942 and 1974.

Stevie Krayer. Publications include two collections of poetry and a translation of Rilke's *The Book of Hours*. She coordinated the Spiritual Hospitality Project, a study of Quaker meetings in Wales, and wrote the project report, *Opening the Door*.

John Lampen has travelled widely working for peace, and his poems are mostly reflections on places he visited. His writings include the Pendle Hill pamphlet *Findings: poets and the crisis of faith*.

J J Lawson Oxford graduate, historian and smallholder, was born, and has always lived, in the Welsh Marches.

Alison Leonard has written fiction and drama for all age groups. She has been an active Quaker all her adult life and in recent years has attended pagan and shamanic gatherings.

Laurence Lerner is a retired academic, was Professor of English at Sussex University for over 20 years, and has taught in many countries: West and South Africa, France, Germany, USA. He has published many critical books and seven volumes of poetry. He is a member of Lewes Quaker Meeting.

Alison Lock is a poet and writer of short fiction as well as a facilitator on the 'Life Writing for Transformation' programme. Her latest publication, *Above the Parapet*, is a collection of short stories.

Robert Maxwell read English at Oxford, where he won the Newdigate Prize for Poetry. His working career started in international mining and ended in health policy and management. For his work at the King's Fund he received the CVO and the CBE.

Dorothy Nimmo (1932-2001). Beginning to write in 1980, Nimmo published six collections of poems and three pamphlets, as well as short stories. She was first an actress, then she brought up four children, gardened, kept goats, and was a professional cook. She was caretaker at Gloucester Friends' Meeting House, and later at Settle FMH.

Maggie Norton South Cumbria Poet Laureate 2007; latest collection *Onions and Other Intentions*, Indigo Dreams Publishing; commissioned videopoems – *Bundle on the Dresser*

and *Making Hay;* radio CD – *Kurt Schwitters, in Praise of Life.*
Children's poetry collection forthcoming.

Emmaline O'Dowd. A Friend for about twenty years, based in
Derby. Teacher of violin and piano. Over the years has also had
work in various magazines, e.g. *Staple, Poetry Nottingham,
Dragonheart*, as Sally, or Sally Ann, Wheeler.

Fiona Owen's collections include *Going Gentle* and *Imagining the
Full Hundred*. Her *Screen of Brightness*, with Meredith Andrea, is
published in 2013 by Cinnamon Press. Fiona teaches for the
Open University, is poetry editor for *Scintilla* and is a Quaker
(Holyhead Local Meeting).

Mark Pasco, whose early experiences were with street homeless
in London, now works with addicts in Bristol. Deeply involved
in running a children's charity, he also writes pen portraits of
local characters.

Meg Peacocke. Born 1930. Published four collections with
Peterloo Poets (*Marginal Land, Selves, Speaking of the Dead* and
In Praise of Aunts) and one (*Caliban Dancing*) with the Shoestring
Press. "The good thing about my life is that I have planted
many trees."

Doreen Pearce: "I have three children and five grandchildren.
Writing is an important part of my life now I am retired. I
became a Quaker last year after attending for several years."

Winifred Rawlins (1907-97). The poet and her sister opened
their house to Jewish refugees in WW2, and at Christmas 1945
welcomed German POWs, waiting to go home, into
Berkhamstead FMH. After the war she moved to live in USA.
She published some seven collections.

Rachel Rees lives in Leicester where she is a member of the
Soundswrite poetry group. She is training for a second career as
a speech and language therapist.

Marilyn Ricci lives in Leicestershire. Her poems have
appeared in many magazines and anthologies. Her pamphlet:
Rebuilding a Number 39 was published by Happenstance Press.
She also writes plays.

Mary Rowlands. "Born into Quakerism, I have lived in
Croydon, Cornwall, Birmingham and Yorkshire, now an Elder

in Kirkbymoorside Meeting. Worked part-time as librarian at Woodbrooke Quaker Study Centre and Ackworth School, alongside our family life, and am now rejoicing in great-grandchildren."

Carol Rowntree Jones. Carol's father W K Rowntree was in the long tradition of Quaker grocers. She writes poetry, essays, short fiction and non-fiction. Her day job is media relations officer for The National Forest.

Sibyl Ruth's most recent poetry collection is *I Could Become That Woman* (Five Leaves, 2003). In 2011 she presented *Listen to them Breathing*, a Radio 4 feature about Quaker poets.

Clive Sansom (1910-1981). Poet and speech educator whose collection *The Witnesses* tells the life of Jesus of Nazareth from the perspective of his gospel contemporaries. Famous for his performance poetry and his verses for children, he was also a committed conservationist. In 1949 he and his poet wife settled in Tasmania.

Brigid Sivill (previously Smith) Harlow Quaker Meeting, also meetings in Colombo and Normandy. Brigid has travelled extensively as an educational consultant for literacy. She was a member of the Falmouth Poetry Group. Now living in Normandy, she is a full-time writer.

Ruth Terrington has published in *Writing Women, Magma, Other Poetry* and *The Friend*, and in competition anthologies of *The National Poetry Competition, Blinking Eye*, and the *Templar, Ware* and *Ver Poets*. Her affinity is with landscapes outer and interior.

Bob Ward lives in North Norfolk. Worked in teacher education, then served as a Quaker Prison Minister. A former Editor of the Quaker Arts magazine *Reynard*. Poems / photography on website: www.bobward.org.uk

Clare Wigzell: "I have always read, taught and written poetry and fit it in with family, work and friends. It is essential to my spiritual life."

Waldo Williams (1904-1971) was one of the leading Welsh-language poets of the 20th century, despite the fact that he did not learn Welsh until the age of seven. He was a teacher, a

Quaker and a peace activist, who was jailed for refusing to pay taxes during the Korean War.

Emily Wills has two collections, *Diverting the Sea* (2000) and *Developing the Negative* (2008), both published by The Rialto. She lives in Gloucestershire where she works part-time as a GP.

Acknowledgements

Thanks are due to the poets or their estates, and the publishers of the relevant magazines, anthologies and collections as set out below.

Every effort has been made to trace copyright holders and include correct acknowledgements, and the editors apologise if errors or omissions remain in this list. They would be grateful to know of any corrections that should be incorporated into future editions.

Gillian ALLNUTT: 'the shawl' from *indwelling*, Bloodaxe Books 2013. 'The Road Home' from *How the Bicycle Shone: New & Selected Poems*, Bloodaxe Books, 2007.

Angela ARNOLD: 'Inhabiting the Door' first published in *Pushing out the Boat, 2012*.

Bryan ASPDEN: 'Nant Honddu' and 'Stonecrop' from *News of the Changes*, Poetry Wales Press, 1984.

Elizabeth BAILEY: 'Martha's Song' first published in *The Friend*.

R V BAILEY: 'With You' from *Credentials*, Oversteps Press, 2012. 'Cautious' first published in *Marking Time*, Peterloo Poets, 2004.

Jennifer BARRACLOUGH: 'The Watch Cottage' from *Whatever you desire*, Oscar's Press 2009 (ed. Mary Jo Bang). 'Cutting the Grass at Woodbrooke' first published in *Quaker Monthly, vol 85, Nov 2006*.

Jackie BARTLETT: 'Memento' first published in *Poetry Nottingham Internationa, 2003*.

Alice BEER: 'On growing old' from *Talking of Pots, People and Points of View*, Poetry pf (2005). 'De Montfort Square' from *Window on the Square*, Soundswrite Press, 2009. By permission of Elizabeth Brandow.

Peter BENNET: 'Augenlicht' first published in *In Your Own Time, the Northern Poetry Workshop anthology*.

Catherine BENSON: 'Being Private' from *Untitled as yet*, Smith/Doorstop, 2013.

Gerard BENSON: 'The Bomber' from *A Good Time*, Smith/Doorstop, 2010.

Basil BUNTING: 'What the Chairman Told Tom' and 'At Briggflatts Meetinghouse' from *Basil Bunting: The Complete Poems*, Bloodaxe Books, 2000 (ed. Richard Caddel).

Helena CHAMBERS: 'The Lost Boys' first published in an anthology of the Open Poetry Competition, the Norwich Writers' Circle, 2010.

Anne CLUYSENAAR: 'There were dark leaves spread out' from *Migrations*, Cinnamon 2011. 'Always', from *From seen to unseen and back*, forthcoming from Cinnamon in 2014, was first published in *Temenos*.

Margaret CROMPTON: 'Occupational Therapy 1879' first published online in *Poetry as Pilgrimage, 2012* (ed. Anna Dear).

Peter DANIELS: 'Being English' first published in *Poetry Wales, Spring 2012.*

Julia DARLING: 'End' from *Sudden Collapses in Public Places*, Arc 2003, 'Apology for absence' from *Apology for Absence*, Arc 2004, by permission of Julia Darling's family.

Ann DRYSDALE: 'Dogs in the Wind' from *Between Dryden and Duffy*, Peterloo Poets, 2005. 'Migrant Workers' first published in *The Price of Gold* anthology, Grey Hen Press, 2012.

U A FANTHORPE: 'Collateral Damage' from *Safe as Houses*, Peterloo, 1995. 'Afterwards' from *Consequences*, Peterloo, 2000. 'Rising Damp' from *Standing To*, Peterloo 1982. All three poems appear in *New and Collected Poems*, Enitharmon, 2010.

Kate FOLEY: 'Tikkun Olam' and 'In Quaker Meeting' from *One Window North*, Shoestring Press, 2012. 'Tikkun Olam' first published in *Scintilla 14.*

Andrew GREAVES: 'Lost Children' first published in *Captured Moments*, Poetry Rivals' Collection, Forward Press, 2012 (ed. Helen Davies).

Philip GROSS: 'The Quakers of Pompeii' from *The Egg of Zero*, Bloodaxe Books 2006. 'Vocable: 14' from *Deep Field*, Bloodaxe Books, 2011. 'Retreat' from *Mappa Mundi*, Bloodaxe Books 2003.

June HALL: 'Funny Devices' first published in *The Parkinson*.

Susanne KNOWLES: 'Fox Dancing' first published in *Reynard*, 1968; later in her collection *The Sea Bell and Other Poems*, Dent, 1968, and subsequently in the Heaney and Hughes anthology, *The Rattle Bag*, Faber, 1985.

Stevie KRAYER: 'Sunbrick Burial Ground' first published in *Scintilla 16*. 'Nothing but' first published in *New Welsh Review*, 2012.

Alison LEONARD: 'Callanish Stone Circle' first published in *Sacred Stones* anthology, Adams Media, Avon, Mass. (ed. Maril Crabtree).

Laurence LERNER: 'Residues' from *Rembrandt's Mirror*, Secker & Warburg, 1987. 'God's Mothers' from *Chapter & Verse: Bible Poems*, Secker & Warburg, 1984.

Alison LOCK: 'Ladybird, Ladybird' from *A Slither of Air*, Indigo Dreams Publishing, 2011.

Robert MAXWELL: 'Ansâri' from *Persian Poems* by Robert Maxwell and Bruce Wannell, Libanus Press, 2012.

Dorothy NIMMO: 'Christmas Poem' was first published under the title *Dark* in *Reynard*, 2001. 'Homewards' from *Giant Steps*, Lancaster, 1987. 'Black Parrot' from *Kill the Black Parrot*, Littlewood Arc, 1993. By permission of The Poetry Business.

Maggie NORTON: 'Opening the Back Door' and 'Christmas on the Lancaster Canal' from *Onions and Other Intentions*, Indigo Dreams Publishing, 2012.

Meg PEACOCKE: 'An Inventory of Silence' from *Caliban Dancing*, Shoestring Press, 2012.

Winifred RAWLINS: 'Man is a Tender Plant' from *Man is a Tender Plant*, Golden Quill Press, USA, 1969.

Rachel REES: 'One son, predeceased' first published in *Poetry Nottingham International*.

Marilyn RICCI: 'Post-Mortem Parenting' was first published in *Other Poetry, Series 4, No 4 2011.*' And when you thought' was previously published in Smiths Knoll, #41, 2007 and *Rebuilding a Number 39*, Happenstance Press, 2008.

Carol ROWNTREE JONES: 'Sensuous, there was nothing sensuous' first published in *The North*.

Clive SANSOM:'The Timeless Hour' from *The Witnesses*, Methuen, 1956.

Ruth TERRINGTON: 'Storing Apples' first published in the National Poetry Competition anthology, 1988. 'The Bird-bit' first published in *Piety and Plum Porridge* competition anthology, Blinking Eye Publishing, 2005.

Bob WARD: 'Fables' from *Trusting at the Last*, Hawthorn Press, 2011; first published in *The Interpreter's House*.

Waldo WILLIAMS: 'Pa beth yw dyn?' and 'Medi' from *Dail Pren* ("Leaves of the Tree"), Gwasg Gomer, 2010. By permission of the estate.